YOUR KNOWLEDGE HAS VALUE

Imprint:

Copyright © 2019 GRIN Verlag
Print and binding: Books on Demand GmbH, Norderstedt Germany
ISBN: 9783346087775

This book at GRIN:

https://www.grin.com/document/510047

Solomon Moses

Theories of Human Memory and Their Application In Education. An Overview

GRIN Verlag

GRIN - Your knowledge has value

Since its foundation in 1998, GRIN has specialized in publishing academic texts by students, college teachers and other academics as e-book and printed book. The website www.grin.com is an ideal platform for presenting term papers, final papers, scientific essays, dissertations and specialist books.

Visit us on the internet:

http://www.grin.com/

http://www.facebook.com/grincom

http://www.twitter.com/grin_com

Table of Contents

INTRODUCTION

How do our memories store information? Why is it that we can recall a memory at will from decades ago, and what purpose does forgetting information served?

Memory has been the subject of investigation among many 20th Century psychologists and remains an active area of study for today's cognitive scientists. Below we take a look at some of the most influential studies, experiments and theories that continue to guide our understanding of the function of the human memory.

Memory," broadly defined, is the ability to use the past in the service of the present. Memory can manifest itself in a variety of ways. When people tie their shoelaces or ride bicycles, they rely on past experiences to execute sequences of motor behaviors that accomplish those tasks. Such skills are often considered examples of *procedural memory*. When people identify objects in the environment (e.g., knowing that a thing is a plant or an animal) or when they give the answer to a factual question, they draw upon stores of general knowledge about the world accumulated over time. This type of memory is often referred to as *semantic memory*. When people remember events, they must attempt to recollect the details of what occurred at a particular place and time. This type of memory is called *episodic memory*.

1. Multi-Store Model (Atkinson & Shiffrin, 1968)

An influential theory of memory known as the multi-store model was proposed by Richard Atkinson and Richard Shiffrin in 1968. This model suggested that information exists in one of 3 states of memory: the sensory, short-term and long-term stores. Information passes from one stage to the next the more we rehearse it in our minds, but can fade away if we do not pay enough attention to it. Information enters the memory from the senses - for instance, the eyes observe a picture, olfactory receptors in the nose might smell coffee or we might hear a piece of music. This stream of information is held in the sensory memory store, and because it consists of a huge amount of data describing our surroundings, we only need to remember a small portion of it. As a result, most sensory information 'decays' and is forgotten after a short period of time. A sight or sound that we might find interesting captures our attention, and our contemplation of this information - known as rehearsal - leads to the data being promoted to the short-term memory store, where it will be held for a few hours or even days in case we need access to it. The short-term memory gives us access to information that is salient to our current situation, but is limited in its capacity. Therefore, we need to further rehearse information in the short-term memory to remember it for longer. This may involve merely recalling and thinking about a past event, or remembering a fact by rote - by thinking or writing about it repeatedly. Rehearsal then further promotes this significant information to the long-term memory store, where Atkinson and Shiffrin believed that it could survive for years, decades or even a lifetime. Key information regarding people that we have met, important life events and other important facts makes it through the sensory and short-term memory stores to reach the long-term memory.

Strengths of Multi Store Theory

One strength of the multistore model is that is gives us a good understanding of the structure and process of the STM. This is good because this allows researchers to expand on this model.

This means researchers can do experiments to improve on this model and make it more valid and they can prove what the stores actually do. Therefore, the model is influential as it has generated a lot of research into memory.

Many memory studies provide evidence to support the distinction between STM and LTM (in terms of encoding, duration and capacity). The model can account for primacy & recency effects.

Weaknesses of Multi Store Theory

The model is oversimplified, in particular when it suggests that both short-term and long-term memory each operate in a single, uniform fashion. We now know is this not the case.

It has now become apparent that both short-term and long-term memory is more complicated than previously thought. For example, the Working Model of Memory proposed by Baddeley and Hitch (1974) showed that short term memory is more than just one simple unitary store and comprises different components (e.g. central executive, Visuospatial etc.).

In the case of long-term memory, it is unlikely that different kinds of knowledge, such as remembering how to play a computer game, the rules of subtraction and remembering what we did yesterday are all stored within a single, long-term memory store.

Indeed different types of long-term memory have been identified, namely episodic (memories of events), procedural (knowledge of how to do things) and semantic (general knowledge).

Rehearsal is considered a too simple explanation to account for the transfer of information from STM to LTM. For instance, the model ignores factors such as motivation, effect and strategy (e.g. mnemonics) which underpin learning.

Also, rehearsal is not essential to transfer information into LTM. For example, why are we able to recall information which we did not rehearse (e.g. swimming) yet unable to recall information which we have rehearsed (e.g. reading your notes while revising).

Therefore, the role of rehearsal as a means of transferring from STM to LTM is much less important than Atkinson and Shiffrin (1968) claimed in their model.

The models main emphasis was on structure and tends to neglect the process elements of memory (e.g. it only focuses on attention and maintenance rehearsal). For example, elaboration rehearsal leads to recall of information than just maintenance rehearsal.

2. Levels of Processing (Craik & Lockhart, 1972)

Fergus Craik and Robert Lockhart were critical of explanation for memory provided by the multi-store model, so in 1972 they proposed an alternative explanation known as the levels of processing effect. According to this model, memories do not reside in 3 stores; instead, the strength of a memory trace depends upon the quality of processing, or rehearsal, of a stimulus. In other words, the more we think about something, the more long-lasting the memory we have of it (Craik & Lockhart, 1972). Craik and Lockhart distinguished between two types of processing that take place when we make an observation: shallow and deep processing.

Shallow processing - considering the overall appearance or sound of something - generally leads to a stimuli being forgotten. This explains why we may walk past many people in the street on a morning commute, but not remember a single face by lunch time.

Deep (or semantic) processing, on the other hand, involves elaborative rehearsal - focusing on a stimulus in a more considered way, such as thinking about the meaning of a word or the

4

consequences of an event. For example, merely reading a news story involves shallow processing, but thinking about the repercussions of the story - how it will affect people - requires deep processing, which increases the likelihood of details of the story being memorized.

Strengths

The theory is an improvement on Atkinson & Shiffrin's account of transfer from STM to LTM. For example, elaboration rehearsal leads to recall of information than just maintenance rehearsal.

The levels of processing model changed the direction of memory research. It showed that encoding was not a simple, straightforward process. This widened the focus from seeing long-term memory as a simple storage unit to seeing it as a complex processing system.

Craik and Lockhart's ideas led to hundreds of experiments, most of which confirmed the superiority of 'deep' semantic processing for remembering information. It explains why we remember some things much better and for much longer than others.

This explanation of memory is useful in everyday life because it highlights the way in which elaboration, which requires deeper processing of information, can aid memory.

Weaknesses

Despite these strengths, there are a number of criticisms of the levels of processing theory:

It does not explain how the deeper processing results in better memories.

Deeper processing takes more effort than shallow processing and it could be this, rather than the depth of processing that makes it more likely people will remember something.

The concept of depth is vague and cannot be observed. Therefore, it cannot be objectively measured.

Eysenck (1990) claims that the level of processing theory describes rather than explains. Craik and Lockhart (1972) argued that deep processing leads to better long-term memory than shallow processing. However, they failed to provide a detailed account of why deep processing is so effective.

The type of processing, the amount of effort & the length of time spent on processing tend to be confounded. Deeper processing goes with more effort and more time, so it is difficult to know which factor influences the results.

The ideas of 'depth' and 'elaboration' are vague and ill defined (Eysenck, 1978). As a result, they are difficult to measure. Indeed, there is no independent way of measuring the depth of processing. This can lead to a circular argument - it is predicted that deeply processed information will be remembered better, but the measure of depth of processing is how well the information is remembered.

The levels of processing theory focuses on the processes involved in memory, and thus ignore the structures. There is evidence to support the idea of memory structures such as STM and LTM as the Multi-Store Model proposed (e.g. H.M., serial position effect etc.). Therefore, memory is more complex than described by the LOP theory.

3. Working Memory Model (Baddeley & Hitch, 1974)

Whilst the Multi-Store Model provided a compelling insight into how sensory information is filtered and made available for recall according to its importance to us, Alan Baddeley and Graham Hitch viewed the short-term memory (STM) store as being over-simplistic and proposed a working memory model (Baddeley & Hitch, 1974), which replaces the STM.

The working memory model proposed 2 components:

a visuo-spatial sketchpad (the 'inner eye') and

an articulatory-phonological loop (the 'inner ear'), which focus on a different types of sensory information. Both work independently of one another, but are regulated by a central executive, which collects and processes information from the other components similarly to how a computer processor handles data held separately on a hard disk.

According to Baddeley and Hitch, the visuo-spatial sketchpad handles visual data - our observations of our surroundings - and spatial information - our understanding of objects' size and location in our environment and their position in relation to ourselves. This enables us to interact with objects: to pick up a drink or avoid walking into a door, for example.

The visuo-spatial sketchpad also enables a person to recall and consider visual information stored in the long-term memory. When you try to recall a friend's face, your ability to visualize their appearance involves the visuo-spatial sketchpad.

The articulatory-phonological loop handles the sounds and voices that we hear. Auditory memory traces are normally forgotten but may be rehearsed using the 'inner voice'; a process which can strengthen our memory of a particular sound.

Strengths

Researchers today generally agree that short-term memory is made up of a number of components or subsystems. The working memory model has replaced the idea of a unitary (one part) STM as suggested by the multistore model.

The working memory model explains a lot more than the multistore model. It makes sense of a range of tasks - verbal reasoning, comprehension, reading, problem-solving and visual and spatial processing. And the model is supported by considerable experimental evidence.

The working memory applies to real-life tasks such as:

i. Reading (phonological loop)

ii. Problem solving (central executive)

iii. Navigation (visual and spatial processing)

Working memory is supported by dual-task studies (Baddeley and Hitch, 1976). The working memory model does not over emphasize the importance of rehearsal for STM retention, in contrast to the multi-store model.

Weaknesses

Lieberman (1980) criticizes the working memory model as the Visuospatial sketchpad (VSS) implies that all spatial information was first visual (they are linked).

However, Lieberman points out that blind people have excellent spatial awareness, although they have never had any visual information. Lieberman argues that the VSS should be separated into two different components: one for visual information and one for spatial.

There is little direct evidence for how the central executive works and what it does. The capacity of the central executive has never been measured.

Working memory only involves STM, so it is not a comprehensive model of memory (as it does not include SM or LTM).

The working memory model does not explain changes in processing ability that occur as the result of practice or time.

4. Miller's Magic Number (Miller, 1956)

Prior to the working memory model, U.S. cognitive psychologist George A. Miller questioned the limits of the short-term memory's capacity. In a renowned 1956 paper published in the journal Psychological Review, Miller cited the results of previous memory experiments, concluding that people tend only to be able to hold, on average, 7 chunks of information (plus or minus two) in the short-term memory before needing to further process them for longer storage. For instance, most people would be able to remember a 7-digit phone number but would struggle to remember a 10-digit number. This led to Miller describing the number 7 +/- 2 as a "magical" number in our understanding of memory.

But why are we able to remember the whole sentence that a friend has just uttered, when it consists of dozens of individual chunks in the form of letters? With a background in linguistics, having studied speech at the University of Alabama, Miller understood that the brain was able to 'chunk' items of information together and that these chunks counted towards the 7-chunk limit of the STM. A long word, for example, consists of many letters, which in turn form numerous phonemes. Instead of only being able to remember a 7-letter word, the mind "recodes" it, chunking the individual items of data together. This process allows us to boost the limits of recollection to a list of 7 separate words.

Miller's understanding of the limits of human memory applies to both the short-term store in the multi-store model and Baddeley and Hitch's working memory. Only through sustained effort of rehearsing information are we able to memorize data for longer than a short period of time.

5. Memory Decay (Peterson and Peterson, 1959)

The Decay theory is a theory that proposes that memory fades due to the mere passage of time. Information is therefore less available for later retrieval as time passes and memory, as well as memory strength, wears away. When an individual learns something new, a neurochemical "memory trace" is created. However, over time this trace slowly disintegrates. Actively rehearsing information is believed to be a major factor counteracting this temporal decline. It is widely believed that neurons die off gradually as we age, yet some older memories can be stronger than most recent memories. Thus, decay theory mostly affects the short-term memory system, meaning that older memories (in long-term memory) are often more resistant to shocks or physical attacks on the brain. It is also thought that the passage of time alone cannot cause forgetting, and that decay theory must also take into account some processes that occur as more time passes. The term "decay theory" was first coined by Edward Thorndike in his book The Psychology of Learning in 1914. This simply states that if a person does not access and use the memory representation they have formed the memory trace will fade or decay over time. This theory was based on the early memory work by Hermann Ebbinghaus in the late 19th century.

Following Miller's 'magic number' paper regarding the capacity of the short-term memory, Peterson and Peterson set out to measure memories' longevity - how long will a memory last without being rehearsed before it is forgotten completely?

In an experiment employing a Brown-Peterson task, participants were given a list of trigrams - meaningless lists of 3 letters (e.g. GRT, PXM, RBZ) - to remember. After the trigrams had been shown, participants were asked to count down from a number, and to recall the trigrams at various periods after remembering them.

The use of such trigrams makes it impracticable for participants to assign meaning to the data to help encode them more easily, while the interference task prevented rehearsal, enabling the researchers to measure the duration of short-term memories more accurately.

Whilst almost all participants were initially able to recall the trigrams, after 18 seconds recall accuracy fell to around just 10%. Peterson and Peterson's study demonstrated the surprising brevity of memories in the short-term store, before decay affects our ability to recall them.

6. Flashbulb Memories (Brown & Kulik, 1977)

There are particular moments in living history that vast numbers of people seem to hold vivid recollections of. You will likely be able to recall such an event that you hold unusually detailed memories of yourself. When many people learned that JFK, Elvis Presley or Princess Diana died, or they heard of the terrorist attacks taking place in New York City in 2001, a detailed memory seems to have formed of what they were doing at the particular moment that they heard such news.

Psychologists Roger Brown and James Kulik recognized this memory phenomenon as early as 1977, when they published a paper describing flashbulb memories - vivid and highly detailed snapshots created often (but not necessarily) at times of shock or trauma.

We are able to recall minute details of our personal circumstances whilst engaging in otherwise mundane activities when we learnt of such events. Moreover, we do not need to be personally connected to an event for it to affect us, and for it lead to the creation of a flashbulb memory.

7. Memory and Smell

The link between memory and sense of smell helps many species - not just humans - to survive. The ability to remember and later recognize smells enables animals to detect the nearby presence of members of the same group, potential prey and predators. But how has this evolutionary advantage survived in modern-day humans?

Researchers at the University of North Carolina tested the olfactory effects on memory encoding and retrieval in a 1989 experiment. Male college students were shown a series of slides of pictures of females, whose attractiveness they were asked to rate on a scale. Whilst viewing the slides, the participants were exposed to pleasant odor of aftershave or an unpleasant smell. Their recollection of the faces in the slides was later tested in an environment containing either the same or a different scent.

The results showed that participants were better able to recall memories when the scent at the time of encoding matched that at the time of recall (Cann and Ross, 1989). These findings suggest that a link between our sense of smell and memories remains, even if it provides less of a survival advantage than it did for our more primitive ancestors.

8. Interference

Interference theory postulates that we forget memories due to other memories interfering with our recall. Interference can be either retroactive or proactive: new information can interfere with older memories (retroactive interference), whilst information we already know can affect our ability to memorize new information (proactive interference).

Both types of interference are more likely to occur when two memories are semantically related, as demonstrated in a 1960 experiment in which two groups of participants were given a list of word pairs to remember, so that they could recall the second 'response' word when given the first as a stimulus. A second group was also given a list to learn, but afterwards was asked to memorize a second list of word pairs. When both groups were asked to recall the words from the first list, those who had just learnt that list were able to recall more words than the group that had learnt a second list (Underwood & Postman, 1960). This supported the concept of retroactive interference: the second list impacted upon memories of words from the first list.

Interference also works in the opposite direction: existing memories sometimes inhibit our ability to memorize new information. This might occur when you receive a work schedule, for instance. When you are given a new schedule a few months later, you may find yourself adhering to the original times. The schedule that you already knew interferes with your memory of the new schedule.

There are two types of interference; retroactive and proactive.

Retroactive interference is when more recent information gets in the way of trying to recall older information. An example would be calling your ex-boyfriend/girlfriend by your new boyfriend/girlfriend's name. The new name retroactively interferes with the old one, which is clearly problematic for recall.

Proactive interference is the reverse direction of interference to retroactive interference. This is when old information prevents the recall of newer information. This could, for example, occur with telephone numbers. When trying to recall a new phone number, the old phone number you have previously had for years could proactively interfere with the recall, to the point when it is very difficult to remember the new number.

Strengths of the theory

Research evidence: There is research to support this theory such as the study from Baddeley and Hitch (1977)

Intuitively correct: Most people can think of times when interference in both directions have occurred. This means that the theory makes sense and there are plenty of everyday examples of it occurring.

Weaknesses of the theory

Limited scope: This theory only can explain lack of recall when information in a similar format prevents recall. This means that there are many types of recall that are not explained by this theory.

Poor ecological validity: Like much of memory research there is a problem with the validity of the research that supports the theory. It is predominantly laboratory based and therefore does not test everyday recall.

9. False Memories

Can false memories be implanted in our minds? The idea may sound like the basis of a dystopian science fiction story, but evidence suggests that memories that we already hold can be manipulated long after their encoding. Moreover, we can even be coerced into believing invented accounts of events to be true, creating false memories that we then accept as our own.

Cognitive psychologist Elizabeth Loftus has spent much of her life researching the reliability of our memories; particularly in circumstances when their accuracy has wider consequences, such as the testimonials of eyewitness in criminal trials. Loftus found that the phrasing of questions used to extract accounts of events can lead witnesses to attest to events inaccurately.

In one experiment, Loftus showed a group of participants a video of a car collision, where the vehicle was travelling at a one of a variety of speeds. She then asked them the car's speed using a sentence whose depiction of the crash was adjusted from mild to severe using different verbs. Loftus found when the question suggested that the crash had been severe, participants disregarded their video observation and vouched that the car had been travelling faster than if the crash had been more of a gentle bump (Loftus and Palmer, 1974). The use of framed questions, as demonstrated by Loftus, can retroactively interfere with existing memories of events.

James Coan (1997) demonstrated that false memories can even be produced of entire events. He produced booklets detailing various childhood events and gave them to family members to read. The booklet given to his brother contained a false account of him being lost in a shopping mall, being found by an older man and then finding his family. When asked to recall the events, Coan's brother believed the lost in a mall story to have actually occurred, and even embellished the account with his own details (Coan, 1997).

10. The Weapon Effect on Eyewitness Testimonies (Johnson & Scott, 1976)

A person's ability to memorize an event inevitably depends not just on rehearsal but also on the attention paid to it at the time it occurred. In a situation such as an bank robbery, you may have other things on your mind besides memorizing the appearance of the perpetrator. But witness's ability to produce a testimony can sometimes be affected by whether or not a gun was involved in a crime. This phenomenon is known as the weapon effect - when a witness is involved in a situation in which a weapon is present, they have been found to remember details less accurately than a similar situation without a weapon.

The weapon effect on eyewitness testimonies was the subject of a 1976 experiment in which participants situated in a waiting room watched as a man left a room carrying a pen in one hand. Another group of participants heard an aggressive argument, and then saw a man leave a room carrying a blood-stained knife.

Later, when asked to identify the man in a line-up, participants who saw the man carrying a weapon were less able to identify him than those who had seen the man carrying a pen (Johnson & Scott, 1976). Witnesses' focus of attention had been distracted by a weapon, impeding their ability to remember other details of the event.

TYPES OF MEMORY

The types are:

Episodic Memory:

Episodic memory is said to be the store of the autobiographical events in the life of the individual and is organized according to the time, space and other qualities of the specific event or events.

What is happening to you now, that of which you are conscious is the reflection of what is being stored in primary and also the current content of the episodic memory. For example, if you come back and narrate about an accident you have witnessed, it is episodic memory.

Semantic Memory:

Semantic memory on the other hand, stores a collection of relationships between events which may or may not have passed through episodic memory but stores the collection of relationships between events. In other words, semantic memory includes the organized knowledge we have about language, i.e. words and other verbal symbols, their memory and the relations between them, rules, formulae and the manipulation of these symbols, concepts and relations.

Procedural Memory:

Sometimes, the term procedural memory is also used in addition to the terms of episodic memory and semantic memory. This is also known as skill memory. Skill memory mainly involves how to do things in a complex operation. For example, when one is driving a car or a scooter, this involves many activities to be carried out in a sequence. In fact, there are many activities which involve a retrieval of learnt and stored up information and this happens in an automatic and unconscious manner.

Type of memory	Degree and kind of encoding	Storage	Retrieval
Sensory memory	Little encoding	Short-term	Mechanical retrieval
Short-term memory	Primary acoustic	Can retain5 to 9 chunks	General scan
Long-term memory	Semantic coding	No limitation	Integration of new material

HOW TO IMPROVE MEMORY

There are certain general principles explaining the ways of improving memory. Here are some suggestions for improving memory:

1. Develop will to remember: While learning anything, one must have strong will to learn and remember. Strong will helps for better understanding and in turn for better memory.

2. Keep concentration: Attention and concentration on the material to be learnt is very important. Concentration helps for better understanding and in turn for better memory.

3. Picturise the learning material/situation: Develop mental picture of the learning situation. The advantage of visual aids is that they facilitate acquisition of visual images. These images come to our memory picture.

4. Use spaced method: Follow spaced or distribution method. Avoid unspaced method, so that a good settlement of learnt material takes place and remains in mind accurately.

5. Avoid shocks and emotional disturbances: Avoid learning while in shock and when emotionally disturbed, because our psychological processes are affected, and hence our memory also.

6. Use learnt material: Disuse causes forgetting.

7. Rhythm as an aid to memory: Try to introduce style and rhythm into whatever you learn.

8. Do not recall when there is some inhibition or resistance: It will be recalled automatically after some time.

9. Over learning is beneficial: Try to read as many times as possible. Experiments have proved that over learning helps better memory.

10. Role of recitation: Recitation has an upper hand over passive reading. This is nothing but rehearsal. Recitation ensures active participation on the part of the learner. This helps in transformation of information from STM to LTM.

11. Take rest or sleep after study: Rest or if possible sleep after a long study will help for fixation and consolidation of learnt material.

12. Get feedback by testing the self, a person will also be practicing his retrieval skills.

13. Develop association: We must try to connect or relate whatever we learn with what we have already learnt well. For example, to remember seven colors of rainbow-we use word VIBGYOR.

14. Mnemonics: This word comes from a Greek word 'nemoniks', which mean assisting the memory. These are memory improvement techniques rely on the linking or association of, to be remembered material with a systematic and organized set of images or words which serve as remainder cues called memory pegs.

They are:

i. Method of loci: The word loci mean places. The memory peg in this system are parts of your image of a scene, which can be a street, tree, big building, etc- with more discrete items to remember.

ii. Rhyming system: The numbers can be used in this system. For example, 1 is a fun, 2 is a shoe, 3 is a tree, 4 is a door, etc. in kindergarten schools, lessons are taught to children by this method only.

iii. Tell stories to yourself: Make a story of unrelated, discrete items. So that remembering a story is very easy. For example, journey taken up by you and places visited, etc.

iv. Chunking: It is a very systematic way of encoding information. Suppose we want to remember a list of long letters or digits, break them into pieces of few words, or letters, or digits which mean something to you-like date of birth, some important incidents, events, etc.

FACTORS THAT INFLUENCE MEMORY

Under this heading, let us examine some factors which influence our memory process. They include the processes to improve retention, remembering and also overcoming forgetting. They are:

i. Ability to retain: This depends upon good memory traces left in the brain by past experiences.

ii. Good health: A person with good health can retain the learnt material better than a person with poor health.

iii. Age of the learner: Youngsters can remember better than the aged.

iv. Maturity: Very young children cannot retain and remember complex material.

v. Will to remember: Willingness to remember helps for better retention.

vi. Intelligence: More intelligent person will have better memory than a dull person,

vii. Interest: If a person has more interest, he will learn and retain better.

viii. Over learning: Experiments have proved that over learning will lead to better memory.

ix. Speed of learning: Quicker learning leads to better retention,

x. Meaningfulness of the material: Meaningful materials remain in our memory for longer period than for nonsense material,

xi. Sleep or rest: Sleep or rest immediately after learning strengthens connections in the brain and helps for clear memory.

How does working memory work in the classroom?

Memory plays a key role in supporting children's learning over the school years, and beyond this into adulthood. It is proposed here that working memory is crucially required to store information while other material is being mentally manipulated during the classroom learning activities that form the foundations for the acquisition of complex skills and knowledge. A child with a poor working memory capacity will struggle and often fail in such activities, disrupting and delaying learning.

CONCLUSION

Memory is central to being human. Imagine your life without memory: you would not know who you are, where you came from, who your family is, what you were doing at any time in the past and what you planned to do after school. So memory can be seen as an anchor to the past, allowing us to understand what is currently happening, and to project ourselves into the future. Understanding how memory works can help us to remember better and can also help us support those whose memory does not work as well as others

REFERENCES

Baddeley, A. (2000). The episodic buffer: a new component of working memory? *Trends in cognitive sciences, 4*(11), 417-423.

Berman, M.G. (2009) In Search of Decay in Verbal Short Term Memory [Electronic Version]. Journal of Experimental Psychology: Learning, Memory, and Cognition, 35(2), pp. 317-333. Retrieved March 6, 2010

Perruchet, P., & Pacton, S. (2006). Implicit learning and statistical learning: One phenomenon, two approaches. *Trends in cognitive sciences, 10*(5), 233-238.

Dienes, Z., & Perner, J. (2002). A theory of the implicit nature of implicit learning. *Implicit learning and consciousness*, 68-92.

Roediger, H. L., Rajaram, S., & Geraci, L. (2007). Three forms of consciousness in retrieving memories. In P. D. Zelazo, M. Moscovitch, & E. Thompson (Eds.), *Cambridge handbook of consciousness* (pp. 251-287). New York: Cambridge University Press.

Tulving, E. (1985). Memory and consciousness. *Canadian Psychology/Psychologie Canadienne, 26*(1), 1.

Conway, M. A. (2005). Memory and the self. *Journal of memory and language, 53*(4), 594-628.

Ghosh, V. E., & Gilboa, A. (2014). What is a memory schema? A historical perspective on current neuroscience literature. *Neuropsychologia, 53*, 104-114.

Moscovitch, M., Nadel, L., Winocur, G., Gilboa, A., & Rosenbaum, R. S. (2006). The cognitive neuroscience of remote episodic, semantic and spatial memory. *Current opinion in neurobiology, 16*(2), 179-190.

Ralph, L., Matthew, A., & Patterson, K. (2008). Generalization and differentiation in semantic memory. *Annals of the New York Academy of Sciences, 1124*(1), 61-76.

Goswami, U. (2011) (Ed.) *Childhood cognitive development Chapter 5*. Wiley-Blackwell.

: Ashby, F. G., & Maddox, W. T. (2005). Human category learning. *Annu. Rev. Psychol.*, *56*, 149-178.

Schank, R. C. (1999). *Dynamic memory revisited Ch2*. Cambridge University Press.

Eichenbaum, H. 2008. *Learning and memory*. New York: W. W. Norton.

Roediger, H. L., ed. 2008. *Learning and memory: A comprehensive reference*. Vol. 2, *Cognitive psychology of memory*. Editor-in-chief: J. Byrne. Oxford: Elsevier.

Roediger, H. L., Y. Dudai, and S. M. Fitzpatrick, eds. 2007. *Science of memory: Concepts*. Oxford: Oxford Univ. Press.

Schacter, D. L. 2001. *The seven sins of memory: How the mind forgets and remembers*. Boston: Houghton Mifflin.